# Baseball's
# HOME-RUN
# HITTERS

The SPORTS HEROES Library

# Baseball's HOME-RUN HITTERS

*Richard Rainbolt*

Lerner Publications Company
Minneapolis

ACKNOWLEDGMENTS

The illustrations are reproduced through the courtesy of: pp. 6, 10, 14, 21, 23, 27, 29, 32, 37, 42, 45, 49, 53, 58, 64, 70, Wide World Photos; pp. 17, 36, 55, National Baseball Library; p. 61, John E. Biever Photos; p. 67, Minnesota Twins.

## Cover photo by Vernon J. Biever

LIBRARY OF CONGRESS CATALOGING IN PUBLICATION DATA

**Rainbolt, Richard.**
Baseball's home-run hitters.

(The Sports Heroes Library)
SUMMARY: Brief biographies emphasizing the careers of ten famous home-run hitters: Babe Ruth, Lou Gehrig, Jimmy Foxx, Ted Williams, Ralph Kiner, Mickey Mantle, Willie Mays, Roger Maris, Henry Aaron, and Harmon Killebrew.

1. Baseball—Biography—Juvenile literature. [1. Baseball—Biography. 2. Batting (Baseball)] I. Title.

GV867.5.R34      796.357′092′2[B][920]      74-27473
ISBN 0-8225-1055-3

**1977 Revised Edition**

Copyright © 1977, 1975 by Lerner Publications Company

All rights reserved. International copyright secured. No part of this book may be reproduced in any form whatsoever without permission in writing from the publisher except for the inclusion of brief quotations in an acknowledged review.

Published simultaneously in Canada by
J. M. Dent & Sons (Canada) Ltd., Don Mills, Ontario

Manufactured in the United States of America

International Standard Book Number: 0-8225-1055-3
Library of Congress Catalog Card Number: 74-27473

Second Printing 1977

## *Contents*

| | |
|---|---|
| Introduction | 7 |
| Babe Ruth | 11 |
| Lou Gehrig | 17 |
| Jimmy Foxx | 23 |
| Ted Williams | 29 |
| Ralph Kiner | 37 |
| Mickey Mantle | 42 |
| Willie Mays | 48 |
| Roger Maris | 55 |
| Henry Aaron | 60 |
| Harmon Killebrew | 66 |

# Introduction

Every sport has its heroes. The heroes of baseball are its home-run hitters. Powerful players blessed with a special sense of timing, they are the idols of young sports fans and often the envy of older ones. They are consistently able to do the hardest thing in the game—hit home runs. Though there are many hitters in baseball, there are few home-run greats. Why? What does it take to be a home-run king? In answering these questions, we must consider several things.

Imagine that we are selecting the foremost home-run hitters in baseball. In doing this, we could look at each player's career batting average and home-run total. But if we were to *rank* the players this way, we would not be getting the whole story. There is much more to deciding the worth of a hitter than adding up his batting scores. It is just as important to look at each player's career history. By doing this, we can get a better look at each man's special talents.

Take Roger Maris, for example. If we were to add up the total number of home runs Maris hit in his career, we would find that he does not rank among the best all-time hitters in baseball. Roger Maris is famous, instead, for setting a new single-season home-run record. In 1961, he hit 61 home runs, a record that has not yet been bettered.

If we look at the career histories of other players, we would find even more interesting facts. Some players, for example, have hit a great number of home runs during very short careers. Obviously, these players could have set some amazing records if they had played baseball longer than they did. Ralph Kiner is an example. He played only 10 years in the major leagues. In that time, he hit just over half as many home runs as Babe Ruth hit during his entire 21-year career. Also, Kiner's season batting average was greater than Ruth's. Perhaps if Kiner had stayed in baseball as long as Ruth, he would have surpassed Ruth's record of 714 home runs.

In choosing baseball's greatest hitters, we should also realize that the tools of the sport have changed over the years. Think back to the days of Babe Ruth and Jimmy Foxx. The baseball they swung at was much different from the baseball of today. It did not go as far when it was hit as today's ball does. This means that home-run stars in the early years of baseball probably had to work harder for what they achieved.

The men whose careers are reviewed in this book are only a few of baseball's all-time greats. Other players who are not included have also earned a special place in baseball history. Among them are Duke Snyder, Stan Musial, Hank Greenberg, Eddie Mathews, Frank Howard, Rocky Colavito, and Ernie Banks. These men and all the other professional players in baseball have made the game one of America's favorites.

*Babe Ruth crosses the plate for the 700th time—July 13, 1934.*

## Babe Ruth

No athlete has had a greater impact on the sport he played than Babe Ruth had on baseball. He was the most popular, the most colorful, and probably the most powerful baseball player of all time. During his career, Babe set records that players are still trying to break today.

Babe was born George Herman Ruth in Baltimore, Maryland, in 1895. As a child, Babe was not given much attention by his parents. He became a rough and tough little boy. He even chewed tobacco before he was 10 years old. Babe was so tough that his parents sent him away to a school for delinquent children. There he became friends with a priest named Father Matthias, who taught him how to play baseball.

Babe Ruth became an outstanding baseball player at the school. He was especially good at pitching and catching. But as he grew taller and gained more weight, Babe became a powerful hitter, too. In his adult years, Babe Ruth stood 6 feet, 2 inches tall and weighed around 220 pounds. It was his large frame that made his swing so powerful.

In 1914, when he was 19 years old, Babe Ruth joined the Baltimore Orioles of the International League as a pitcher. But shortly after he joined the Orioles, the Boston Red Sox of the American League saw him play, and they bought him. The Red Sox then sent him to their minor-league team for training. Babe spent most of that first season in the minor leagues. But he was called back to play for the Red Sox in the last five games. A year later, in 1915, he played with the Sox for the entire season, most of the time as a pitcher. Babe also hit his first major-league home runs that year—four of them.

If Babe Ruth had not been such a great hitter, he probably would have become one of the game's greatest left-handed pitchers. During his early years in baseball, Ruth won 92 games and lost only 44 as a pitcher. But when the Red Sox realized what a good hitter he was, they began to use him less as a pitcher and more as an outfielder. During the 1918 season, Babe hit 11 home runs to tie for the league lead. A year later, Babe broke that major-league home-run record. He slammed 29 balls either into the stands or over them. To baseball experts of the time, 29 home runs in one season were unbelievable. But that record was nothing compared to what Babe would do in the years to come.

In 1919, one of the most important events in Babe's career took place. He was traded to another team. The Red Sox were having money problems that year. To solve those problems, the Sox decided to sell Babe to another team. Babe Ruth had become a valuable player since he had broken a home-run record. So the Sox knew that they would get a lot of money by selling him. It was the New York Yankees who bought Babe. They paid the Sox $125,000 for him. In those days, $125,000 was a lot of money to pay for a player. But with a home-run slugger like Babe Ruth attracting the crowds, the Yankees got their money back quickly.

In 1921, his first season with the Yanks, Babe amazed the baseball world by smashing out 54 home runs. That was more home runs than the total made by *all the players* on any other team. Over the next two seasons, more than a million fans poured into the Yankee baseball field—the Polo Grounds in New York City. They were eager to see Babe Ruth slam his bat into a ball and send it almost out of sight.

The Yankees moved from the Polo Grounds into their own stadium in 1923. Although it was called Yankee Stadium, the building became known as "The House That Ruth Built." He "built" the stadium by attracting millions of fans to watch him play. But he also did plenty to tear the stadium down, by sending baseballs crashing into walls and bleachers. That first season in the new stadium, Babe managed to get only 41 home runs. But his batting average was a great .393.

Babe Ruth was 33 years old when the Yankees opened their 1927 season. At the time, the experts thought that Ruth's best playing days were over. But they forgot that another slugger—Lou Gehrig—had been moved next to Babe in the batting line-up. This meant that the opposing pitchers could no longer pitch *around* Babe by walking him. Gehrig was a slugger who could hit the Babe home if he was walked. So the pitchers were forced to throw good pitches to the Babe and try to strike him out. But that was not easy. Both Ruth and Gehrig scored off the pitchers' attempts so well, that the Yankees set a record of 110 victories in 1927. And Babe broke his own season home-run record of 59 by hitting 60.

Of Babe Ruth's hundreds of career home runs, the most dramatic was the one he hit during the 1932 World Series in Chicago against the Chicago Cubs. There were bad feelings at the time between Ruth and the Chicago players. The Chicago fans jeered at Babe as he went to bat in the top of the fifth inning. Two strikes were called on Babe, and the jeering grew louder. In a surprise move, Babe stepped away from the plate and pointed his bat at the center field bleachers. Then he stepped back to the plate and slammed the next pitch right to where he had pointed—the center field bleachers.

Age finally caught up with the Babe. In 1934, he dropped to a .288 average with only 22 home runs batted in. The Yankees let him go after that season, but Babe was not ready to quit baseball. He played one more year, with Boston of the National League, and then he retired. In 1948, he died of cancer at the age of 53.

Babe Ruth left baseball with a lifetime home-run total of 714 and a batting average of .342. His records were long the best in baseball history. But even today, after those records have been bettered, American baseball fans still think of Babe Ruth as the all-time greatest.

## Lou Gehrig

When thinking back to the days of Babe Ruth and the New York Yankees, it is only natural to think of Lou Gehrig, too. Gehrig was the Yankees' first baseman. He was also a powerful hitter at the plate. Though not as skilled as his friend and teammate Babe Ruth, Gehrig was just as popular. He loved baseball and always worked hard to do well for the team. When he was finally forced to leave baseball because of a serious illness, the whole country was sad.

Lou Gehrig was born in New York City in 1903. Because his family was poor, Lou had to start working early in his life. He took part-time work after school and brought his earnings home to his mother. But he also found time for sports. In the streets of New York, he became quite good at baseball and football.

After Lou graduated from high school, he entered Columbia University. There he played on the baseball team as a pitcher and an outfielder. It was at a college baseball game that a scout for the New York Yankees saw Gehrig play. The scout reported to the Yankees that he had found another Babe Ruth.

The Yankees probably found it hard to believe that there *could* be another Babe Ruth. But Gehrig sounded good to them, so they offered him

$1,500 to sign a contract. Lou gladly accepted the Yankees' offer because his father had to have an operation and the family needed the money.

When Lou Gehrig first took the field at the Yankee training camp, he was quite clumsy. A big guy —6-feet-1, 210 pounds—Lou had a hard time coordinating his moves on the field. But when he stepped into the batting cage, things were different. As he picked up one of Babe Ruth's bats, the Yankee players started to heckle him. But Lou was confident as the pitcher wound up and threw the ball. His first swing sent the ball deep into the right field bleachers. Until then, that area had received only *Ruth's* grand slams.

Lou's first year in the majors was 1923. He went to bat only 26 times for the Yankees, cracking out 11 hits for a .423 average. He also made his first big-league home run that season.

Lou did not become a regular with the Yankees until the 1925 season. On June 2 of that year, the Yankee's regular first baseman, Wally Pipp, told the manager that he had a headache. Pipp was told to take a rest, and Gehrig was sent in to replace him for a day or so. But Lou covered first base so well that he stayed at that position for the next 14 years without missing a game. At bat in 1925, Lou slugged 21 home runs for a .295 average. The following year, 1926, Lou raised his batting average to .313, though he made only 16 home runs.

Had Lou Gehrig played for any other team at any other time, he might have won greater fame in baseball. But as a New York Yankee during the 1920s and 1930s, Lou Gehrig always played in the shadow of the mighty Babe Ruth. Because of this, Gehrig's own great plays were often overlooked. But Lou did not mind. He once said that he was just not the kind of guy who wanted to make newspaper headlines.

In spite of playing in the Babe's long shadow, Lou Gehrig did some pretty unusual things in baseball. During one game, he hit four home runs and almost hit a fifth. (The fifth hit was stopped by the outfield fence.) And two times he hit 49 homers in a single season. These were things that few other players, if any, had ever done before.

Gehrig also established a baseball record for most consecutive games played (most games played in a row). In all, Lou played 2,130 consecutive games. The fans could always count on seeing him play. He played even when he did not feel well. Once, his unbelievable consecutive game streak almost came to an end when a high fever kept him from playing. But a Yankee official saved the day. Seeing a single cloud in the sky, the man called the game off because of "bad weather."

All went well for Lou until 1938. During that season, Lou seemed to have trouble with his coordination. He stumbled often and sometimes even fell down. In the spring of 1939, the change was even more noticeable. He seemed to have lost all of his power at the plate. His fielding was also poor. His playing was just not as good as it usually was. And no one was more worried about

*Babe Ruth (right) shows his affection for his friend and teammate Lou Gehrig before thousands of cheering fans. Lou Gehrig Day at Yankee Stadium — July 4, 1939.*

it than Lou himself. He tried all the harder to do well, but he just couldn't. Finally, on May 2, 1939, Lou told the Yankee manager that he wanted to be taken out of the lineup. He said that he was no longer helping the ball club. He also felt that people were feeling sorry for him, and he did not want that. So Lou Gehrig put himself on the bench and ended his long, unbroken record of attendance on his team.

A month later, June 1939, the Yankees sent Lou to the famous Mayo Clinic in Minnesota for a physical checkup. The doctors there found that "The Iron Horse," the man who always kept himself in top physical shape, had a rare disease. And it was a disease that could not be cured. The whole world soon learned that the great Lou Gehrig was dying.

On July 4, 1939, the Yankees held a Lou Gehrig Day in Yankee Stadium. Thousands of people from all over the country came to honor the great athlete. All the early Yankee stars were there, too. Babe Ruth spoke of his long and close partnership with Lou and cried openly. Lou's other teammates and friends also made speeches. Lou stood by, humbly listening to the kind words of tribute. He cried too as he gave a short speech of thanks.

Lou Gehrig died just two years later, in 1941.

## Jimmy Foxx

Until the 1960s, Jimmy Foxx ranked second only to Babe Ruth in career home runs. Like Babe, Jimmy Foxx was a large man who had a tremendously powerful swing. A right-handed hitter, Jimmy stood just under 6 feet tall and weighed 200 pounds. It is said that he could hit a baseball with as much power as Babe Ruth.

Jimmy Foxx was born in Sudlersville, Maryland, in 1907. As a young boy on his father's farm, Jimmy always had plenty of chores to do. It was probably the hard farm work that made him the powerful baseball player he later became. Among his teammates, Foxx was known as "The Maryland Strongboy," or simply, "The Beast."

Jimmy Foxx broke into professional baseball in 1924 at the age of 16. It happened when his skill in high school baseball was seen by the scout of a minor-league team. Eager to play pro ball, Foxx dropped out of high school to join the team. His performance during his first season was very good for a 16-year-old. By 1925, Jimmy Foxx had made it into the major leagues with the Philadelphia Athletics. Over the next two years, Foxx went through his training period. As time passed, he went to bat more and more often. And he played many positions in order to find his place on the team.

In 1928, Foxx became a regular on the Athletics team. In the field, he was sent to cover first base. At bat that year, Foxx hit only 13 home runs for a .328 average. But in 1929, he hit over twice as many homers—33.

It was not until 1932 that Jimmy challenged the single-season home-run record then held by Babe Ruth. (Ruth had hit 60 home runs in 1927.) Foxx might even have set a new record, too, if several unfortunate things had not happened to prevent it. Three times that season Jimmy hit long drives, but they were stopped by new screens on top of the outfield fences. He hit home runs early in two other games. But rain stopped each game, and the runs were wiped from the record book. Foxx finished the 1932 season with a total of 58 runs, not including the 5 homers he *might* have had.

The Maryland Strongboy continued his battle with the fences during the next three seasons. And he did well, too. Foxx drove in 48 homers in 1933, 44 in 1934, and 36 in 1935. In spite of this show of power, the Athletics traded Foxx to the Boston Red Sox at the end of the 1935 season. They did this because money problems were forcing them to sell their best players.

Foxx's best year with the Red Sox was 1938. He hit 50 homers for a .349 average and a total of

175 runs batted in. Foxx had only two good home-run seasons after that. He hit 35 home runs in 1939 and 36 in 1940. In 1941, he managed only 19. It was clear that Jimmy Foxx was nearing the end of his home-run years.

In 1942, Foxx had five homers to his credit when the Red Sox released him on waivers to the Chicago Cubs. He hit three home runs for the Cubs during the rest of the 1942 season.

Foxx's career as a hitter may not have been helped by the fact that he played many different positions. At various times he had been a catcher, a first baseman, and a third baseman. And in his last season in the major leagues, he even agreed to try pitching. This happened in 1945 when he was with the Philadelphia Phillies.

By 1945, Jimmy's reflexes at the plate had slowed down so much that he was no longer helping the team as a hitter. During that season he hit only seven home runs for the Phillies. Foxx was still as strong as he had always been, though. And when he tried pitching, it was found that he could fire a baseball with great speed. After that, the Phillies used Foxx as a relief pitcher often.

Shortly before the start of one game, the Phillies' manager asked Foxx if he would go out as the *starting* pitcher. The agreeable Foxx said that he would

*On August 16, 1940, Jimmy Foxx hit his 495th career home run, bettering Lou Gehrig's 494 to move into second place behind Babe Ruth.*

give his best. After five innings, Jimmy had the fans buzzing, for he had allowed no hits. But when he gave up a hit in the sixth inning, the manager removed him from the game. The Phillies went on to win that game, making Foxx the winning pitcher. All in all, he pitched in nine games in 1945, wining one and losing none. Jimmy Foxx thus became one of the few major-league players to have a perfect winning record as a pitcher. It was an unusual way for one of baseball's great home-run hitters to end his career. For 1945 was Jimmy Foxx's last year in pro baseball.

In 1951 Jimmy Foxx was elected to the Baseball Hall of Fame. He had been such a feared and respected hitter in his time that he had received over 100 bases on balls. And he still holds the record for having been walked six times in one game.

Foxx, who was often called the "right-handed Babe Ruth," died in Florida in 1967.

## Ted Williams

Three things made Ted Williams one of the greatest hitters of all time: his eyes, his magnificent swing, and, most important of all, his determination. He did not settle for just getting into the major leagues of baseball. Ted Williams wanted to be known as baseball's greatest hitter. And he tried hard to become just that. Williams developed what other baseball people called a "flawless" swing. (In other words, there was not one thing wrong with the way he batted.) He did it by studying batting methods. And then he practiced, practiced, practiced. Ted Williams may have been the best student of hitting ever to play baseball.

Even though Ted Williams did become a famous player, his years in baseball were stormy ones. They were marked by many battles—with fans, managers, baseball club owners, and sportswriters. This was because Ted had a hot temper and talked back to almost everyone. He made some enemies that way.

Ted Williams was born in California in 1918. Even as a boy, Ted knew that he wanted to play professional baseball someday. He started his career early. After graduating from high school, Ted signed with the San Diego Padres of the Pacific Coast League as a pitcher and an outfielder. But when the Padres sent him in to pitch the first time, the other team scored several runs. It was decided that Ted would be a better outfielder than a pitcher.

The following year, 1937, Ted Williams was bought by the Boston Red Sox. He went to spring training with the team but was then sent to the Sox's minor-league Minneapolis team. It seemed that the Sox thought he needed more practice. At Minneapolis, Williams hit 43 home runs for an outstanding .366 average. But there was trouble between Williams and his manager. It got so bad that the manager told the club's owner if Williams did not go, *he* would. The owner was able to smooth things over, and both men stayed.

Ted stayed with the Minneapolis team only that one year. He was called back to the Red Sox for the next season. He started his long, successful career in the major leagues by hitting .327 and smashing 31 home runs. His second year with Boston was even better, and his average rose to .344. But the greatest of his seasons was yet to come.

In 1941, Williams got a fast start on his best baseball season. By midseason he had a batting average of .405. This was a special achievement because no other player had hit over .400 since 1930. At the All-Star game, Ted crashed a long home run that won the contest for his team.

Through the last half of the 1941 season, he continued to belt out hits. He hit home runs at a rate of 4 in every 10 times at bat. But then, with only a few games left in the season, Ted's average dropped to an even .400. So that there would be no chance of dropping below the .400 mark, Ted's manager said he should not play the remaining games. But the stubborn and confident Williams said that he would play. He went on to get 6 hits in his last 8 times at bat. And his final season average stood at .406. That was the last time any major-league player has hit .400 or above.

In 1942, Ted Williams won titles for highest batting average, greatest number of home runs, and greatest number of runs batted in (RBIs) in the American League. Together, these titles are known as the triple crown, three baseball awards that few players have ever won all at once. After winning this honor, Williams joined the Marine Corps and served in World War II as a fighter pilot. His baseball career was postponed for the next three years by the war.

It was the Marine doctors who first took notice of Ted's remarkable eyesight. His vision was so rare in quality that only 1 out of 100,000 people had eyesight as good. Because of his excellent vision, Ted became such a good pilot that the Marine Corps made him a teacher of flying.

After the war, Ted Williams continued his baseball career. He played for about six years, and then the Korean War broke out. In 1951, the Marine Corps called Ted back into active duty. He was sent to Korea, where he again served as a pilot. Once, after a dangerous mission, he brought his crippled plane in for a successful belly-flop landing. The event made him something of a hero among his baseball fans in America.

After two years in Korea, Williams returned home to his baseball career. He still had his perfect swing and his good eyesight. And he was still an outstanding hitter. He was so good, in fact, that opposing teams tried to stop him from getting hits. The Cleveland Indians found a way to stop Ted—at least part of the time. They moved all of their infielders to right field when Williams came to bat. They did this because Ted was a great left-handed pull hitter who usually hit the ball down the right field line. By moving to right field, the Indians were able to pick off many of Ted's hits, thus hurting his game.

Most of the other teams in the league used the same shift of fielders against Williams. But Williams himself never did anything about it. He could have sent his hits into left field, but he was a proud and stubborn man who liked to try to get around the fielders. He continued to hit into right field, and it hurt his average. Even so, in 1956, when he was 38 years old, Ted batted a remarkable .388 and hit 38 home runs.

During his career, Ted Williams won six American League batting championships and hit a total of 521 home runs. The final run came in his last time at bat in 1960 at Boston's Fenway Park. Ted was 42 years old, but he batted .317 and hit 29 home runs in that last season.

Ted Williams was never able to beat Babe Ruth's

single-season home-run record of 60. His own greatest single-season record was 43 home runs. Just the same, Williams was one of the best home-run hitters in baseball. And he had missed a total of five seasons to military service. Baseball experts have figured out that if Ted had played those five seasons, he could have hit about 670 career home runs—only 44 short of Babe Ruth's lifetime record.

## Ralph Kiner

Baseball players know that fans would rather see one home run than a lot of base hits during a game. But players have their own ideas about what they want to hit. Some like to make many base hits and establish high batting averages. Others want the fame and money that come from successfully swinging for the fences. Though that is the hardest and most uncertain way to fame, most players try for it. Former baseball slugger Ralph Kiner was one who tried.

There was nothing special about the way Kiner played baseball. He was a slow runner and an average outfielder. But he had a lot of skill with the bat, and he made good use of it. During his 10 short years in the major leagues, Kiner hit 369 home runs. That was an average of almost 37 per season. Babe Ruth's average was less than 33 home runs per season.

Ralph Kiner was born in 1922 in New Mexico, but he grew up in California. He went to school there and became a good athlete in many sports. In baseball, he had average skills except for his power at the plate. Kiner was such a strong hitter that major-league scouts started to take note of him. When he graduated from high school in 1940, many teams offered him contracts. The best offer came from the Pittsburgh Pirates of the National League, and Ralph took it.

Like most players who sign pro baseball contracts, Ralph Kiner went first to a minor-league team for training. He played in the minors from 1941 to 1943 and established himself as a hitter. In 1941, and again in 1942, Kiner was named to his league's All-Star team. In 1942, he led his league in home runs with 14.

Kiner enlisted in the navy in 1943 and served for two and a half years. When he returned to training camp with the Pirates in the spring of 1946, he found that he could hit much better. Now bigger and stronger, Kiner was no longer the kid who had joined the pros five years earlier. The 1946 season was his first in the majors, and he wanted to prove his hitting skills again. Kiner finished the season with a poor .247 batting average and 109 strikeouts. But he led the entire league in home runs with 23.

After his rather slow first season, Kiner came

*Ralph Kiner heads for first after smashing out a single in a game against Boston, 1947.*

back in 1947 and surprised baseball experts by making a serious run at Babe Ruth's season home-run record. He might even have broken it if he had not gotten off to another slow start. As it was, he did not begin to pile up the homers until midsummer. But then he really took off. During one hitting streak, he clubbed 8 home runs in just four games. When the season ended, Kiner had hit 51 home runs, just 9 short of the record 60.

After that terrific 1947 season, Ralph Kiner really began to draw the crowds. The Pirates decided that if the fans were going to pay money to see Kiner hit homers, they would pay him big money to hit them. As a result, Kiner's salary rose to $90,000 a season. This was at a time when players with good batting averages were not even making *half* that much.

In 1948 Ralph Kiner dropped off to 40 homers. But he came back in 1949 to play his best season. He hit 54 home runs and batted an impressive .310.

When it came to hitting home runs, Kiner seemed to have a sense of the dramatic. Selected to play in the All-Star game for three years in a row, he made fantastic hits in each game. In 1949, he belted a two-run homer. In the 1950 All-Star game, he came to bat in the ninth inning with his team behind by one point. The pitch was good, and Kiner drove the ball into the stands to tie the game and send it into extra innings. His National League team later won the game. In the 1951 All-Star game, Kiner belted a homer that helped the National League win its first back-to-back victories against the American League.

Ralph Kiner was the Pirates' only crowd pleaser during his eight years with the club. But in spite of this, the Pirates traded him to the Chicago Cubs in

1953. Following the 1954 season, the Cubs traded Kiner to the Cleveland Indians of the American League.

Ralph Kiner retired from pro baseball in 1955. During his 10-year career, he had achieved a reputation as one of the leading sluggers of all time. For seven seasons—from 1946 to 1953—he led the National League in home runs. And he was one of the few players to approach Babe Ruth's season home-run record. In 1975, when he was 52 years old, Kiner received a former baseball player's greatest tribute—acceptance into the Baseball Hall of Fame.

**Mickey Mantle**

Baseball people will always wonder how good Mickey Mantle could have been if he had not been bothered by injuries much of his career. Mantle played even when he was injured, and that was most of the time. Because of this, it was said that Mantle was able to give only two-thirds of his ability. But Mickey Mantle performing at even two-thirds of his ability was a player to be admired. He could bat either right-handed or left-handed with tremendous power. And his mighty home runs were just as fantastic as Babe Ruth's had been. In 1953, during a game in Washington, Mickey sent a long drive deep over the center field bleachers. The distance was later measured at 565 feet from home plate. Only Babe Ruth had hit a ball that far before.

Mickey Mantle was born in Oklahoma in 1932. Like most young boys, he loved sports and was very active in them. In high school, Mickey made a name for himself as a football player. But he paid for it with injuries. One of them, an ankle injury, would cause him a lot of trouble during his baseball career years later.

Though football was his main sport in high school, Mickey liked baseball more. He had learned the game from his father, who had once played as a semi-professional (not quite a pro, but better than an amateur). It was Mr. Mantle who forced Mickey to learn to hit both right- and left-handed. Those lessons eventually paid off in a big way. When Mickey was still a teen-ager, a New York Yankees scout saw him play on a local team and knew that he would be a good addition to the Yankees team.

Mickey Mantle became a major-league player in 1951 at the age of 19. When he first arrived in the big city of New York, he was shy and a little afraid. He never quite got over this feeling. And he also never got used to being interviewed by writers and television people. But the feelings did not get in the way of his playing. Baseball fans across the country quickly learned that when Mantle stepped to the plate, exciting things happened.

Mickey's unusual hitting power came from his strong arms and his tremendous back muscles. This power made him more than a great hitter—it also made him a fielder of unusual speed. In the outfield, Mantle played alongside the great Joe DiMaggio.

In 1956, and again in 1957, Mickey was named Most Valuable Player in the American League. He led the Yankees to one title after another. In 1956, he won the triple crown by batting .353 with 52 home runs and 130 runs batted in. And in 1957, he hit the best average of his career—.365.

Mantle's achievements over his 18-year career were quite special in the history of baseball. The things he did were even more special when one thinks of the pain he was in much of the time. All through his pro career, Mickey suffered from injuries. His legs were the hardest hit. In 1951, at the start of his career, Mickey injured a leg when he caught his foot in a drainage ditch while chasing a fly ball. His knee was badly damaged, and the leg was never really strong again. After this injury, Mickey used his good leg more, in order to save the weak one. But the constant strain on the good leg made *it* go bad too. The Yankee star then had to have several operations. The operations left Mickey with no cartilage in either of his knees. When he started to play again, Mickey often had his legs wrapped in tape to ease the pain.

In spite of his injuries, Mantle never gave up. In 1961 he made a try at breaking Babe Ruth's single-season home-run record of 60. Trying for that record at the same time was Mickey's roommate and close friend, Roger Maris. The two sluggers put up quite a fight until illness put Mickey out of the race. Mickey had hit 53 home runs—7 away from the record 60—when he got an infection that took him out of the lineup. He was in the hospital when Roger Maris socked his 61st home run to break the Babe's record.

Injuries and illness often limited Mickey's playing ability. But sometimes Mickey limited his own playing by trying too hard and by being too hard on himself. If he was not playing as well as he thought he should, Mickey would become angry with himself and brood. As his feelings changed, so would his batting. This caused him to hit in streaks. But when he *was* in a hitting streak, it was really something to see.

During Mickey's last years in the majors, his crippled legs kept him from playing outfield. So he played first base for a time. Finally, in 1969, it became too painful for him even to go to bat and swing. He retired that year, leaving pro baseball as one of the best loved players in the country. In 1974, Mickey Mantle was elected to the Baseball Hall of Fame.

## *Willie Mays*

Because of his many skills—hitting, fielding, throwing, catching, and base running—Willie Mays was one of the most exciting baseball players in the history of the game. He ranks third among the top home-run hitters of all time. But baseball experts do not think that hitting was Willie's greatest gift. His other skills were so spectacular that his home runs seemed almost ordinary.

Willie Mays was born in Alabama in 1931. From his earliest days, Willie loved baseball. He first played the game for money when he was 14. A few years later, when he was playing with a black team in Birmingham, Willie was discovered by a scout for the New York Giants. He signed a contract with the Giants and was sent to their minor-league team in Trenton, New Jersey, for the 1950 baseball season. He did very well there. The following year he was sent to Minneapolis, the top farm club in the American Association. Willie tore up the league in

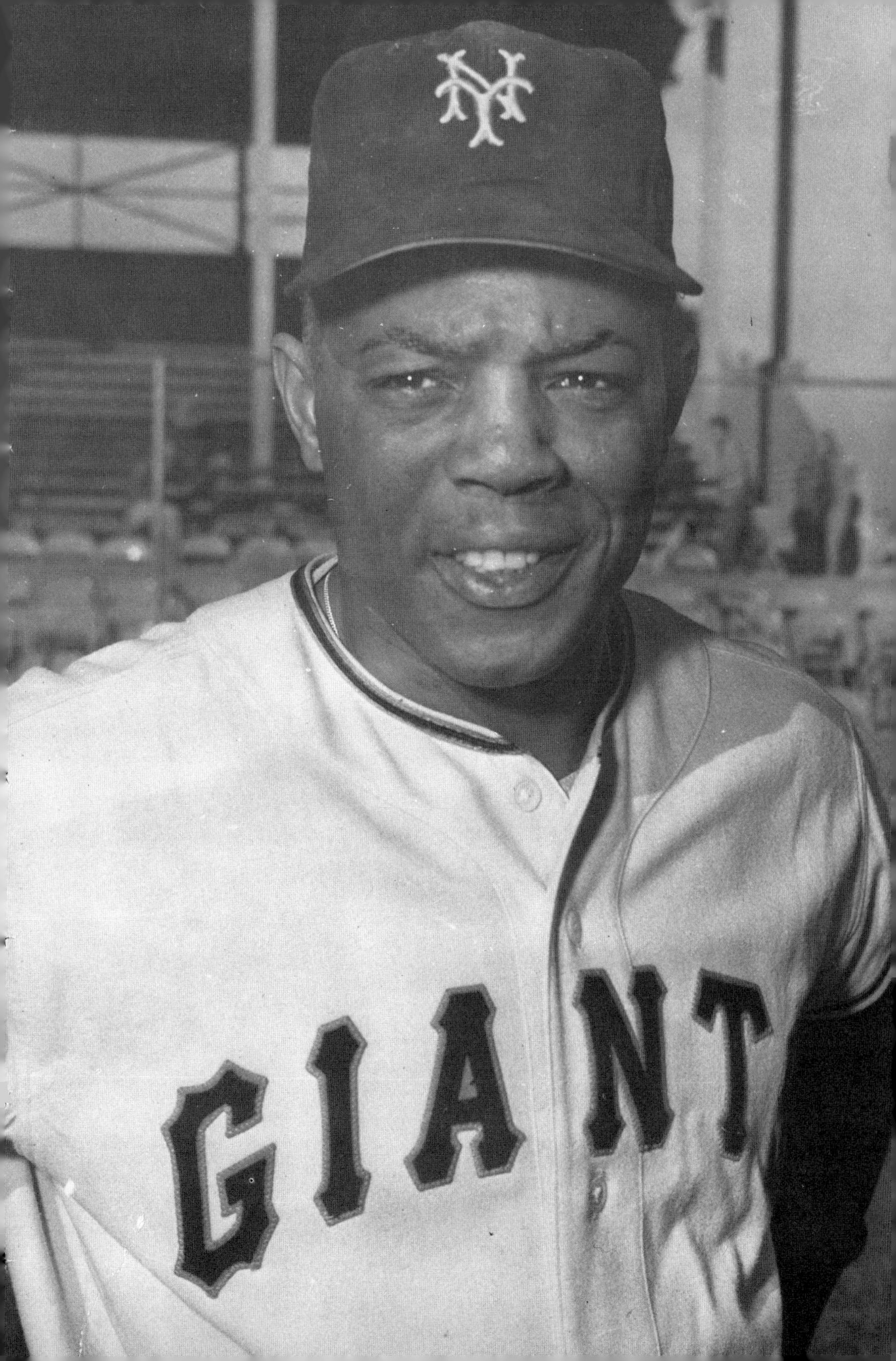
GIANT

the first 35 games of the season, batting an incredible .477 average.

The Giants could not let Willie waste that kind of talent in the minor leagues. So in 1951 they called him back to New York. The 20-year-old was nervous, and he started badly as a result. Through his first several games, Mays just couldn't seem to get it together. But with the help of his manager and close friend Leo Durocher, Mays overcame his fear and lack of confidence.

In 1951, Willie's first year with the Giants, the team was in a race for the pennant. The Giants were trailing the first-place Brooklyn Dodgers by 13 and a half games late in the season. But in the final weeks, the Giants shot ahead of the Dodgers and beat them out of the title. Some say that it was Willie who fired up the Giants for this comeback. That season, after a slow start, Willie smacked out 20 home runs and batted .274 with 68 runs batted in.

The way Willie Mays played baseball said a lot about the kind of person he was. He played hard and well, and at the same time he had a lot of fun doing it. That was because he loved the game so much. A lively, friendly person, Willie was popular among both players and fans. He especially liked kids. Often, when he returned to his New

York City apartment after a game, he would play stickball in the street with the neighborhood kids. Willie was a big, happy kid himself.

During 1952 and 1953 Willie was in the army, serving in Korea. Without him the Giants failed to repeat as pennant winners. But in 1954, Willie was discharged from the army in time to make spring training. No sooner had he arrived at training camp than he was sent to bat in a practice game. Happy to have a bat in his hands again, he drilled the ball out of the park and raised the Giants' hopes for a try at the National League title.

Try they did, and with the peppery Willie leading the way. That 1954 season was Willie's greatest so far. He hit 41 home runs and batted .345. The Giants won the pennant once again. And Willie Mays was named Most Valuable Player in the National League.

In the 1954 World Series game against Cleveland—which the Giants won—Willie made one of his unbelievable catches from his position in center field. At the crack of the bat, he turned his back on home plate and began to race for the fence. The ball went deeper and deeper toward the fence, and so did Willie. He didn't look back until the very minute the ball came down over his shoulder and settled into his outstretched glove. In almost the same motion, he whirled and made a perfect throw back to the infield.

In another game, a runner was on third waiting to score when Willie made a similar catch. Dashing to the outfield after the hit, Willie caught the ball, twisted around without a pause, and threw the ball to the catcher. The surprised runner was tagged out at home plate.

The Giants started to skid after 1954. Mays alone could not keep the team at the top of the National League. In 1955, Willie slammed 51 home runs— his personal high. But his team did not win the pennant that year, nor did they win it during the next two years.

At the end of the 1957 season, the Giants made a big move. Leaving New York City, the team moved across the country to become the San Francisco Giants. Willie did not like this move. He loved the fans in New York, and they loved him too. Mays did not play as well in San Francisco as he had played in New York. But he was his old self when the Giants played in other cities.

For the next 10 years, Mays played consistently fine baseball. He established hitting records in All-Star game events. He helped the Giants win another pennant. And he continued to slug homers and to make good use of his other baseball skills.

One of Willie's greatest moments in baseball came in 1966. He hit his 535th home run to move ahead of Jimmy Foxx and become the second greatest home-run hitter of all time. For a while, it looked as though Willie was going to reach Ruth's record and pass it. But age caught up with him first. By the end of the 1960s, Willie had started to slow down. Then, in 1972, Henry Aaron shot ahead of Willie in the race for the Babe's record. That ended Willie's chances for good.

The year 1972 was another important one for

Willie Mays. With the Giants in a slump and Mays winding down, the Giants decided to trade Willie to the New York Mets. Everyone was happy about the trade—especially Willie and his longtime fans in New York. So Willie Mays went home to New York, where he had always been the happiest. He agreed to stay with the Mets as long as he remained a help to the team. In his first game with the Mets, Willie hit the ball out of the park. But in the following games, he found himself slowed down by leg trouble and other injuries.

At the end of the 1973 season, after 22 years in baseball, Mays retired. On September 25, 1973, over 53,000 fans gathered to honor Willie as their favorite player. There were speeches, gifts, and standing ovations. The fans' farewell was a fitting tribute to the player who had given so much of himself, for so long, to the sport of baseball.

# Roger Maris

Roger Maris does not rank among the top home-run hitters in terms of total hits. He ranks among them instead by being the first player to break one of Babe Ruth's batting records—the single-season home-run record. Maris' record, however, has been argued over by baseball fans for years. That is because he had eight extra season games in which to beat Babe's record.

Roger Maris was born in Hibbing, Minnesota, in 1934. As a young boy, he moved with his family to Fargo, North Dakota. There he went to school and became active in sports. His early favorite was hockey. In high school, however, he was a star football player. His athletic skills earned him many college scholarship offers. But he turned them down because he wanted to play professional baseball.

Roger Maris' baseball career started in 1953 when he signed with the Cleveland Indians of the American League. In those days, Maris was a hot-headed youth who gave his managers a hard time; he sometimes refused to go to the minor-league teams they sent him to for training. But whether he wanted to or not, Roger was forced to spend several seasons in the minor leagues. Then, in 1957, he was called back to Cleveland to play with the pro team. But he missed much of that

*All eyes are on the ball as Roger Maris slams his record-breaking 61st season home run. October 1, 1961.*

season because of injuries. At year's end, his record stood at 14 home runs with an average of .235.

The following year, 1958, Maris was traded to the Kansas City Athletics. He did slightly better there, hitting 28 home runs for an average of .240. In 1959, he batted .273 and hit only 16 home runs.

During the winter of 1959, Kansas City traded Maris to the New York Yankees. There he played in Yankee Stadium—"The House That Ruth Built" —and held an outfield position next to the great home-run slugger Mickey Mantle. Many fans felt that Mantle would be the player to go after Ruth's season home-run record.

There had never been any sign that Maris would try for the same record. His best season home-run total until then had been 32. And that had happened back in 1954, while he was playing in the minors. But in 1960, during his first season with New York, Maris reached a new high of 39 home runs with 112 runs batted in and a .283 average. He even carried the Yankees through the first half of the season while Mantle was out with an injury. As a result, Roger received the league's Most Valuable Player award. Still, Mantle beat him in home runs that season with 40.

The 1961 baseball season did not start out to be an especially memorable one. Maris did not hit his first home run until the 10th game. His next hits were a long time in coming, too. But as the summer moved on, both Maris and Mantle began to swing regularly for the fences. It soon became clear that both of them were in a race to overtake Babe Ruth's record of 60 season homers.

In August 1961, Maris began to pull away from Mantle. And a month later, he hit his 56th home run of the season. The 59th homer came in the 154th game. If 1961 had been a traditional 154-game season, this would have been the end of

Maris' try at the home-run record. But 1961 was the first year of a new 162-game schedule. So Maris had 8 more games in which to hit 61 home runs. The record-breaking 61st homer came in the last game of the season. And Maris was again voted Most Valuable Player in the league.

Because Maris did not achieve what Ruth did in 154 games, many people felt that Maris' record did not count and that Babe's should remain. Today, *both* season totals are considered to be records.

The 1966 season was Maris' last with the New York Yankees. He was traded to the St. Louis Cardinals in 1967. That year he helped the Cards win the National League pennant.

At the end of the 1968 season, Roger Maris retired from pro baseball as the single-season home-run king. No other player has yet come close to taking that title from him.

*Henry Aaron*

On April 8, 1974, Henry Aaron broke the baseball record that experts had once thought was impossible to break—Babe Ruth's lifetime home-run total of 714. When Aaron hit his 715th homer that April day, he broke a record that had stood undefeated for 40 years. During those years, several other famous sluggers had come close to tying the record, but none of them had reached it. Then Hank Aaron came along and did the "impossible." After breaking Babe Ruth's record, Aaron went on to hit many more home runs. When he retired, his lifetime home-run total stood at 755— 41 up on Babe Ruth's old record!

Born in Mobile, Alabama, in 1934, Henry Aaron grew up playing baseball. He was the neighborhood slugger and the envy of his teammates. Later, in school, Hank even skipped classes to watch the pro games. It was his big dream to play pro baseball himself someday. But in the meantime, he worked on improving his skills. In addition to baseball, Hank played football well. He even won a college scholarship for his football skills. But he turned it

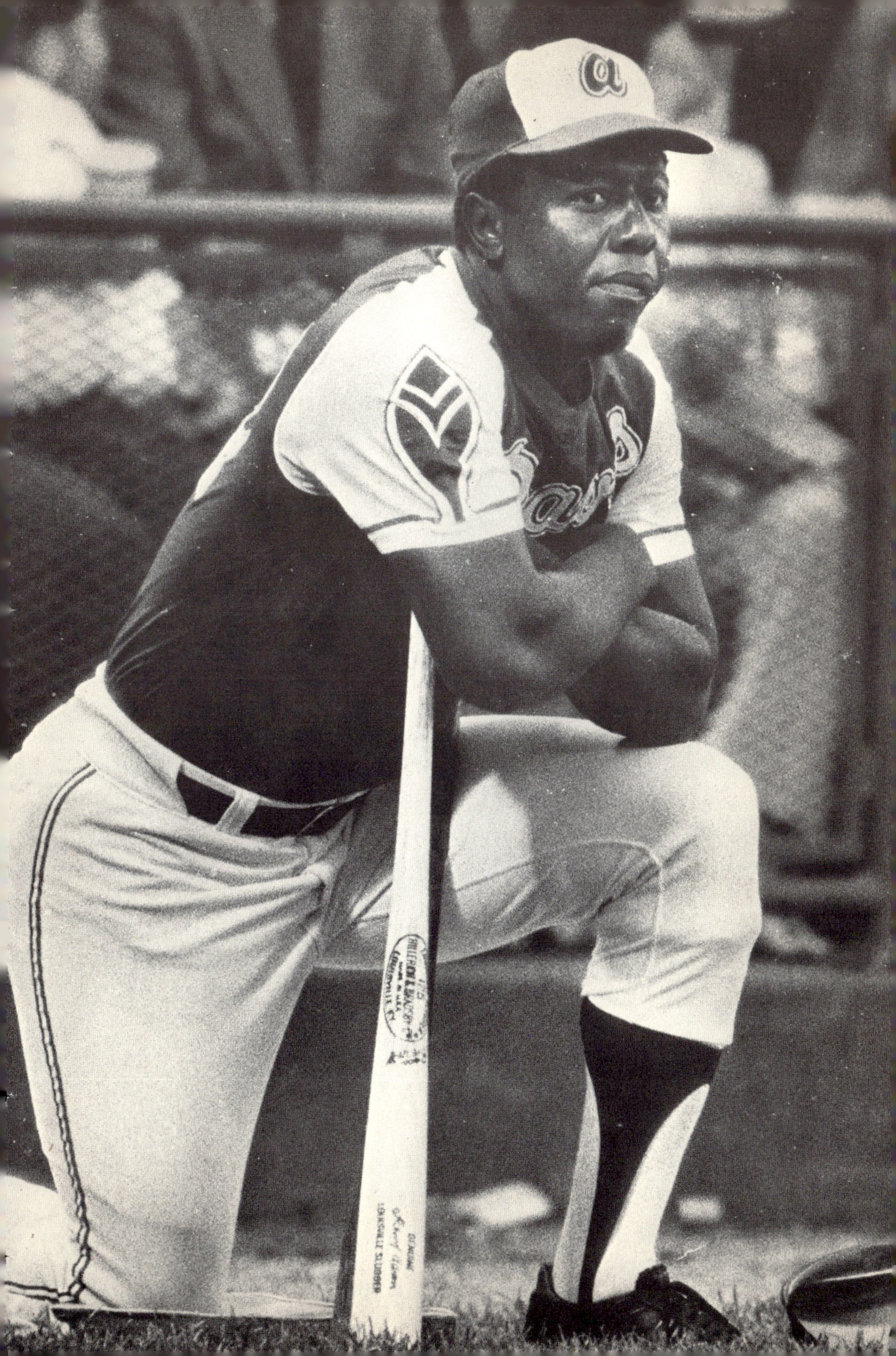

down because major-league baseball was the only game he wanted to play.

In 1952, when he was 18, Hank went to training camp with the Indianapolis Clowns, a pro team of the Negro American League. It seemed to Hank a good place to be spotted by major-league scouts. Hank knew that he did not have to worry about the color barrier in baseball anymore. Just five years earlier, in 1947, Jackie Robinson had become the first black man to play in the major leagues. Now, in 1952, major-league baseball scouts were searching the black leagues for more talent.

One day it happened. A Boston Braves scout was in the stands watching a doubleheader between the Clowns and another team. Aaron played shortstop in both games. In 11 times at bat, he slammed out 10 hits. After seeing Hank play, the scout wasted no time in getting his name on a contract.

Like most starting major-league players, Hank Aaron had to spend some time in training. Boston sent him to its minor-league team in Eau Claire, Wisconsin, for the 1952 season, and to Jacksonville, Florida, for the 1953 season. Hank led the league in hitting at Jacksonville, but as an infielder he was not very good. So he was switched to the outfield, where he was to play for most of his career.

In 1954, Hank played his first season with the

Braves. At the time, the Braves had just moved from Boston to Milwaukee and were considered to be a promising team. They had many good players. Twenty-year-old Hank Aaron knew that he could do well too, if given the chance. From the start, however, he was sent in to bat only as a pinch hitter. But one day, player Bobby Thomson broke an ankle, and Hank was sent in to take his place. Over the next few months, the rookie worked hard to make a place for himself in the lineup. By September, Hank had hit 13 home runs and had batted .280 before he too broke an ankle and was put on the sidelines.

In 1955, Hank Aaron raised his average to .314 and belted out 27 homers. Since then, Hank has been a consistently good hitter—the best the game has ever known. In 1956 and again in 1959, he held the league batting title. In 1957 he earned the league's Most Valuable Player award. That year he also helped the Milwaukee Braves win their first National League pennant, as well as their first World Series. In 1958, Aaron led his team to its second pennant. And four times—in 1957, 1963, 1966, and 1967—he led the league in home runs.

By the end of 1966, the year the Braves moved from Milwaukee to Atlanta, Hank had hit his 400th home run. His 600th homer came in 1971, and his

700th in 1973. The run that tied Ruth's record came early in 1974, when Hank hit his 714th career home run. Then, on April 8, 1974, he hit the big one, the record-breaking 715th home run. In achieving that total, Hank had hit from 30 to 40 runs each season for 20 years. This pace established him as the most consistent hitter in baseball history.

*A jubilant Henry Aaron faces newsmen after hitting the big one—number 715.*

By the end of the 1974 baseball season, Hank Aaron had hit 733 home runs. He was planning to retire, but then an exciting new opportunity opened up for him. That opportunity became a reality when Hank was traded to the Milwaukee Brewers as a designated hitter. Hank was delighted about the trade, for it enabled him to return to the city where he had begun his career as a major-league player. Hank had come a long way since 1954, when he was a pinch hitter for the Milwaukee Braves.

What was the key to Hank Aaron's success? It was due partly to his excellent physical condition, partly to his quiet, simple life-style, and partly to his unique style of hitting. Though Aaron was not as large as many of the other great sluggers, he was a power hitter. He did not overpower a pitch by throwing his weight into the swing. Aaron's power came instead from the swift snap of his strong wrists as he strode into a pitch and drilled the ball out of the park.

When Hank retired as a player after the 1976 season, his home-run career total stood at a remarkable 755. What is more, his total for runs batted in stood at 2,297. These major-league records may *never* be equaled, much less broken. As long as they stand undefeated, Hank Aaron will remain the "king of the home-run hitters."

## *Harmon Killebrew*

Of all the great baseball players included in this book, Harmon Killebrew was surely one of the most respected and best liked. Not only was he a top home-run hitter, but he was also a modest man who went out of his way to help others. His only "enemies," if he had any at all, might have been some of the American League pitchers who feared throwing to the powerful slugger.

Born in 1937 in Payette, Idaho, Harmon Killebrew became an outstanding athlete during his school years. He was a strong, well-built young man who played football, basketball, and baseball very well. But it was his long home runs in baseball that attracted attention. Scouts from various major-league teams tried to sign Harmon up after he graduated from high school. But Harmon had been offered a college scholarship, and he felt that he should take it. When the Washington Senators offered Harmon $30,000 to sign with them, however, he accepted their offer.

Harmon was just a 17-year-old country boy when

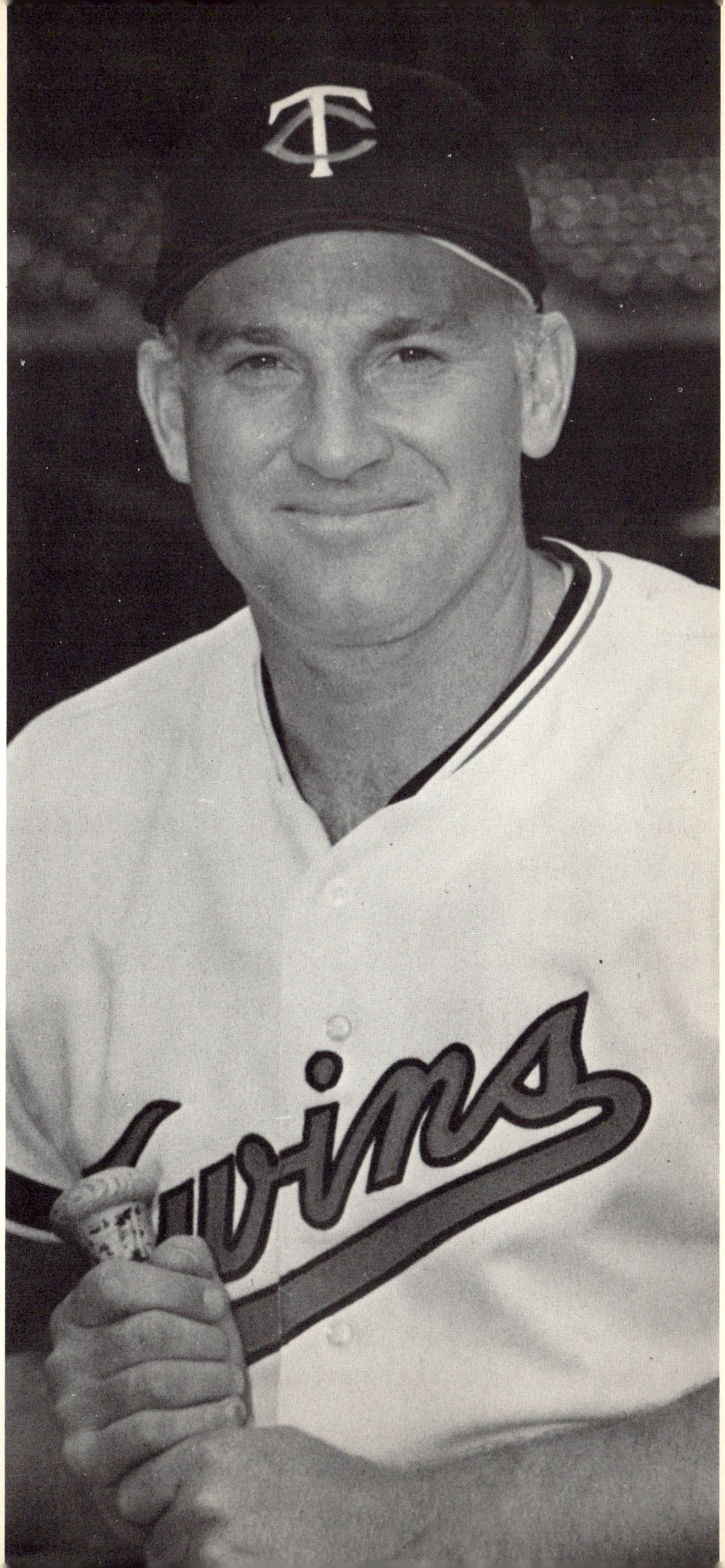
Twins

he joined the Senators in 1954. Though he had the skills, his game needed a lot of improvement before he could break into Washington's lineup. Harmon spent a lot of time practicing. During the games, he spent a lot of time on the bench. But during the 1955 season, he played a few games with the Senators and hit his first major-league home run. He slammed that ball 475 feet into the bleachers, surprising everyone with his power.

For a time after that, however, it did not seem as though the boy from Idaho was living up to his ability. Though he was a terrific hitter, his hits were few and far between. Also, his fielding was not very good. The Washington manager did not even think Harmon was a good enough fielder to make it in the majors.

For more training, Harmon was sent to various minor-league farm teams. He did well in the minors, but when he was called back to the Senators, he did not do as well. For five seasons, Harmon traveled back and forth between Washington and the minor-league teams. For a while, he thought of quitting baseball. Then, in 1959, the Senators decided they would give him a chance to play as a regular.

Harmon played third base in the season opener and stayed in that position the rest of the season.

Though his fielding did not improve very much, he made up for it with his hits. The homers started coming slowly at first, but then they happened quite often. Harmon had found his groove. He was soon hitting at a pace that began to challenge Babe Ruth's season home-run record! By midseason, Harmon was ahead of Babe's pace for the record year. But he slumped badly in the second half of the season. Even so, Harmon finished his rookie year with 42 home runs. That record put him in a tie for the league title.

Harmon Killebrew suddenly became famous. The manager of another major-league team was so impressed with Killebrew that he offered Washington half a million dollars for him. But the Senators turned the offer down; Harmon was drawing fans by the thousands with his mighty hits. When the Senators moved to Minnesota in 1961 to become the Minnesota Twins, Harmon helped draw more than a million new fans to the park. He hit 46 home runs that season. A year later, in 1962, Harmon led the American League in home runs with 48, and RBIs with 126.

Harmon Killebrew was fast earning the nickname "The Killer" because of his long, powerful drives. The power behind those hits was due to his strong wrists and muscular arms. Standing just

*Harmon Killebrew safe at home*

under 6 feet tall and weighing over 200 pounds, Killebrew was one of the strongest home-run hitters of all time. He once powered a baseball some 520 feet into the stands. And many of his hits traveled well over 400 feet.

Even though he was strong, Killebrew was slowed down from time to time by injuries. Each time, he worked hard not to let his injury affect his game. In 1963, he missed 20 games because of a knee sprain. Later that season, while the knee was still healing, he pulled a hamstring muscle in his leg. Both injuries caused him a lot of pain, but he played anyway. That season he managed to hit 45 homers and win the title for the second year in a row. In 1964, Harmon bounced back from knee surgery to win the home-run title again.

Harmon Killebrew finished the 1967 baseball season in a tie for the season home-run title with 44 hits. But in 1968, he suffered a serious hamstring injury that reduced his home-run output to just 17. That winter, Harmon exercised in order to strengthen his body for the 1969 season. He returned in 1969 to hit 49 home runs and 140 RBIs, becoming league leader in both categories. For his achievements, Harmon was named the American League's Most Valuable Player.

Through the early 1970s, Harmon continued to be one of baseball's top power hitters. By the end of 1974, his career home-run total stood at 559, a record that placed him first among American League hitters and fifth overall. Killebrew looked forward to another season as a designated hitter for the Twins. But when the team offered him a less important position, he left the Twins and signed a contract with the Kansas City Royals.

Harmon Killebrew retired as a player after finishing the 1975 season with the Royals. He then began a career as a television sports announcer. The popular baseball great will long be remembered—not only as an outstanding hitter, but also as a dedicated athlete who contributed much to his sport.

## *About the Author*

Richard Rainbolt is a longtime sports fan who has written a number of lively, well-received sports books. Among them are *Gold Glory*, a history of the Minnesota Gophers; *The Goldy Shuffle*, the story of Bill Goldsworthy of the Minnesota North Stars; and *The Minnesota Vikings*, a fast-paced history of that famous team. As one might guess from his books, the author is a native of Minnesota. After serving in the U.S. Marines, Mr. Rainbolt attended the University of Minnesota, where he received a degree in journalism. Since then, he has worked as a newspaper reporter, a public relations man, and a reporter for the Associated Press. In addition to writing, Mr. Rainbolt now runs his own public relations firm.